FIRST CODING

CODING

DEBUGGING CODE

By Sam Thompson

Gareth Stevens
PUBLISHING

Please visit our website, www.garethstevens.com. For a free color catalog of all our high-quality books, call toll free 1-800-542-2595 or fax 1-877-542-2596.

Cataloging-in-Publication Data
Names: Thompson, Sam.
Title: Debugging code / Sam Thompson.
Description: New York : Gareth Stevens, 2022. | Series: First coding | Includes glossary and index.
Identifiers: ISBN 9781538274392 (pbk.) | ISBN 9781538274415 (library bound) | ISBN 9781538274408 (6 pack) | ISBN 9781538274422 (ebook)
Subjects: LCSH: Debugging in computer science–Juvenile literature. | Coding theory–Juvenile literature. | Computer programming–Juvenile literature.
Classification: LCC QA76.9.D43 T466 2022 | DDC 004.2'4–dc23

Published in 2022 by
Gareth Stevens Publishing
29 E. 21st Street
New York, NY 10010

Written by: Sam Thompson
Edited by: Madeline Tyler
Designed by: Dan Scase

Printed in the United States of America

CPSIA compliance information: Batch #CWGS22: For further information contact Gareth Stevens, New York, New York at 1-800-542-2595.

Find us on

Photo credits

All images are courtesy of Shutterstock.com. With thanks to Getty Images, Thinkstock Photo and iStockphoto. Front cover – Patrick Foto, – RoryDesign, the_same_space, Lineicons freebird, Happy Art, RaulAlmu, airdone. 4&5 – myboys.me, AlesiaKan. 4&5 – jamesteohart, AlesiaKan. 6&7 – BEST-BACKGROUNDS, LightField Studios. 8&9 – Gorodenkoff, Bogdan Vija. 10&11 – Morrowind, U.S. Naval Historical Center Online Library. 12&13 – Jacob Lund, sonia.eps. 14&15 – Mr.Note19, Daniel Krason, FrameStockFootages, Darren Brode, Noch. 16&17 – RomanBykhalets, Abscent, Blablo101, Serg036. 18&19 – REDPIXEL.PL. 20&21 – Chaosamran_Studio, Stasique, dnaveh, MSSA. 22&23 – Naval History and Heritage Command, The Turing Digital Archive, tulpahn. Background on all pages – magic pictures. Tablet – Olga Lebedeva. Icons – RoryDesign, the_same_space, Lineicons freebird, Happy Art, RaulAlmu.

CONTENTS

Words that look like this can be found in the glossary on page 24.

WHAT IS CODING?

Coding means telling a computer what to do by writing a set of <u>instructions</u>. The set of instructions is called a code. We use coding to do all sorts of amazing things on a computer.

Another name for coding is programming.

A computer is a machine that can follow instructions and <u>store</u> information.

Information is the numbers and facts that tell you about something.

Someone who writes code is called a programmer.

Bits of information are put together to make a program. The program is then <u>run</u> on a computer.

WHY CODE?

Coding lets you control computers. If you could code, you could make programs and websites that do whatever you want. What would you make your website about?

Computers are an important part of life. In the future, we will need lots of people who can code because there will be even more computers.

You may be able to teach your grown-ups to code!

FOLLOWING STEPS

Computers are very good at following instructions. However, they are not very good at thinking for themselves. This means that a piece of code needs to tell a computer exactly what to do.

Computers can carry out millions of instructions every second.

However, if the code is wrong or has parts that are missing, the computer will do the wrong thing. Even small mistakes can make a computer do the wrong thing, or not work at all.

Always check that your code is right.

WHAT ARE BUGS?

Bugs are mistakes in a code. There are lots of different kinds of mistakes, and some bugs are worse than others.

9/9

0800   antan started
1000   "   stopped - antan ✓   { 1.2700   9.037 847 025
        13"uc (032) MP - MC   9.037 846 795 cor
                                        1.682 ...000
                                        2.130476415 (3) 4.615925059 (-2
        (033)   PRO 2   2.130476415
                conect   2.130676415
        Relays 6-2 in 033 failed special speed test
        In relay   "   " 10,000 test .
                Relays changed
1100   Started Cosine Tape (Sine check)
1525   Started Mult + Adder Test.

1545   Relay #70 Panel F
                                    (moth) in relay.

        First actual case of bug being found.
1630 antangent started.
1700 closed down .

A real bug!

In the 1940s, a programmer named Grace Hopper found a real bug in a machine. This was the first time a bug had been caused by a real bug!

11

WHAT IS DEBUGGING?

Taking the bugs out of code is called debugging. When debugging, the programmers test their code again and again to find bugs. Then they carefully read through the code to take any mistakes out.

Bugs are part of programming. Nobody is perfect, so there will always be some problems with the code. The most important thing is that the big mistakes are fixed.

Talking out loud can help you spot problems. Some programmers find that it helps to explain the code to a rubber duck!

PLAYTESTING

When video games are made, they need to be tested a lot. This is called playtesting. Games are very complicated, and there can be lots of bugs.

Someone who tests video games is called a playtester.

For some people, it is their whole job to test video games. Playtesters need to play a game, or part of a game, again and again to find any problems. Then they tell the programmer, who tries to fix the code.

COMMON BUGS

There are lots of different types of bugs.

Fatal Error

⊗ **Error!**

OK

Some bugs are caused because the instructions are impossible. For example, some math sums might be impossible to work out. If these sums are put in the code, the program might not work.

Code is made up of certain words and <u>symbols</u>. If the words or symbols are typed wrong or in the wrong order, this can cause a program to <u>crash</u>.

Sometimes, the programmer doesn't realize what their code will do. The program might not crash, but if it does something that the programmer didn't expect, that is still a bug.

COMMENTS

Programmers can add comments to their code. Comments are part of the code that the program won't read. Programmers can leave notes for each other in the code which won't confuse the computer.

Comments can help explain the code to other people.

Programmers use different symbols to tell computers which parts of the code are comments. The symbols are different for different <u>programming languages</u>.

In many programming languages, short comments are written after two forward slashes (//).

WHAT CAN CODING DO?

Coding can make all sorts of programs. Some of these programs are used to draw and make pictures. Other programs can create <u>animations</u> and films.

Animation was once done by hand. Now, most people use computers.

Every app you have ever used has been made using code. Apps such as games or video players are usually made by huge teams of programmers.

FAMOUS PROGRAMMERS

GRACE HOPPER

Mathematician and Computer Programmer

Grace Hopper joined the U.S. Navy as a computer programmer. She helped <u>develop</u> some very important early computer technology. She also found the first bug, as you may remember from page 11!

ALAN TURING

Mathematician and Code Breaker

Alan Turing made one of the first electronic computers. His work is still very important for computers today. In <u>World War Two</u>, he cracked an important code that helped the <u>Allies</u> win the war.

GLOSSARY

Allies	a group of countries that were on the same side during World War Two
animations	films that use lots of images that are put together and played quickly to make it look like something is moving
crash	(in computers) when a program stops working
develop	work on something so that it grows or becomes better
instructions	a set of steps that explain how something is done
programming languages	languages that humans use to write instructions for computers
run	when a computer reads through all the instructions and does what it is told
store	keep in order to use later
symbols	things that are used as a sign of something else
World War Two	a war fought between 1939 and 1945

INDEX